# JUST PLANT SEEDS

## A MESSAGE OF HOPE FOR RELIGIOUS EDUCATORS

### JARED DEES

---

For more information, visit jareddees.com.

Paperback: ISBN 978-1-954135-10-9
eBook: ISBN 978-1-954135-11-6

*For the members of*

*TheReligionTeacher.com*

# CONTENTS

## D IS FOR DISCIPLINE

## S IS FOR SAYINGS

# JUST PLANT

In his letter to the Corinthians, Saint Paul said something every overwhelmed religious educator should remember:

> "I planted, Apollos watered, but God gave the growth."
>
> —1 Corinthians 3:6

Saint Paul planted seeds.

Apollos watered the seeds.

God gave the growth.

We are not God. God will enable the faith inside the hearts of young people to grow. Don't worry about that part of the journey. God has it under control. The growth is not our responsibility. Just plant the seeds.

We are not Apollos. You and I only get to see our students for a limited amount of time each week. We only get to teach them for a year, then they move on to the next grade and the next teacher and the next phase of life. They are going to have an Apollos to help their faith blossom. But you? You are not Apollos. You are just planting seeds.

We are Saint Paul. Saint Paul was a planter. He planted seeds of faith in the lives of many people in many different cities. We know this because he wrote letters to these churches in Rome, Galatia, Philippi, Thessalonica, and Corinth. He was a missionary and moved from one place to the next. He was a starter, not a finisher.

Most of the time as a religious educator, you don't get to see the seeds grow. You don't get to see the fruits of your labor. You don't get to see what happens to the students you teach. You may never know if they become dedicated Christians or not. Instead, you will find joy in the planting.

Just plant seeds and let God and others do the rest.

# GROWING WITH GOD

Let's read it again:

> "I planted, Apollos watered, but God gave the growth."

> —1 Corinthians 3:6

Think back on your life and each new stage you grew into along the way. Think about the different homes, schools, cities, churches, and communities you lived in over the years. Each new place brought new people. Teachers came and went, as did coaches and many of your friends. Some people are still with you, but maybe not in the same way.

So, what's left after all those different stops along the way? The people came and went, but God was there with you every step of the way. People and places passed away, but God was there all along.

Remember that famous story about the footprints in the sand? A person walks along the beach with God and sees many scenes of his or her life. There were footprints in the sand for each scene.

*In each scene, I noticed footprints in the sand. Sometimes there were two sets of footprints; other times there was only one set of footprints.*

*During the low periods of my life, I could see only one set of footprints. So, I said, "You promised me, Lord, that you would walk with me always. Why, when I have needed you most, have you not been there for me?"*

*The Lord replied, "The times when you have seen only one set of footprints, my child, is when I carried you."*

God gives the growth. At every part of your life, God was there for you. God was with you and helping you get through the good times and the bad. Even when it felt like you were all alone like the one set of footprints in the sand, know that God was right there with you carrying you along the way. He has always been there and he will always be with you.

Here's the point: God will be with your students through every challenge they face this year. He will be with them long after they have grown and gone on to the next stage of life. God will carry them through all that he has in store for them. "In the wilderness, where you saw how the Lord your God carried you, just as one carries a child, all the way that you have traveled until you reached this place" (Dt 1:31).

Take comfort in all these changes and challenges. We cannot be with our students forever, but we know that God is with them always. They will continue to grow like plants in a garden as God encourages them to grow through both good times and bad. We can put our trust in God to give the growth. All we must do is show up with

4

joy and trust in God that he will take care of the young people we serve.

Just plant seeds. Let God give the growth. Let God carry them like a child all the days of their lives.

# LET GO OF THE ANXIETY

The responsibility of religious education can be overwhelming. There is an overwhelming number of things to do and topics to teach. We can feel overwhelmed by feelings of failure—for not teaching enough, not reaching enough kids, not making a big enough impact. We can be overwhelmed by lack of class participation or misbehaviors, not to mention the additional stress in our personal lives.

But remember what Jesus said:

"Come to me, all you that are weary and carrying heavy burdens, and I will give you rest. Take my yoke upon you, and learn from me; for I am gentle and humble in heart, and you will find rest for your souls. For my yoke is easy, and my burden is light" (Mt 11:28-30).

Feeling overwhelmed stems from a lack of control in your life. It's understandable. When we feel in control, we feel that life is manageable. But when life feels out of control, we become anxious and overwhelmed.

Meditate on these words!

Jesus says, when you feel overwhelmed "come to me." Come to him when you feel heavy burdens. Start there. Turn to him, not to yourself to work harder. You cannot beat yourself up anymore for not making a big enough difference in the lives of your students.

Jesus also says, "take my yoke upon you" and "my burden is light." Well, it certainly doesn't feel that way, does it? But think about this. We take up the yoke of service like an ox pulls a plow. Our responsibility is only to serve, not to succeed.

God is the one that gives the growth. The outcomes are secondary to the service. Think about all the stressful experiences you have had lately: unsuccessful lessons and activities, misbehaving kids, rude comments, running out of time to teach, missing materials, etc. Turn your stress into service. We are just here to plant the seeds and let God take it from there. We cannot and will not ever be able to control the outcome. But we can control the effort.

Just plant seeds. Pull the plow. Let go of the outcome and let God do the rest.

# REALITY CHECK

Do you remember the names of all your teachers? First grade? Second grade? How about seventh grade or high school? It might get hard to remember them all.

How about your students? Do you remember the names of all the students you have ever taught? The longer you do this work, the harder it is to remember everyone. At this point, I have taught close to 1,000 students. It would not be humanly possible to sit down and list all 1,000 names of those children, many of whom are grown up and with children of their own now.

Here's a reality check for you. Many of your students will not remember your name. Some of them may only have vague memories of their time with you. This goes for both schoolteachers and catechists. The hard truth is that we won't always be remembered.

And you know what? That's okay.

It's okay if your students forget you. Your work is not about you. The work is about God.

We are planting seeds now. The seeds will grow, and God will continue to enable that growth. So what if they forget us? We are here to plant seeds of faith through the stories, experiences, emotions, and ideas we share. We leave the rest up to God to grow their faith now that the seeds have been planted.

Just plant seeds. It's okay if the kids forget who sowed those seeds in the first place.

# YOUR TEACHING IS NOT YOUR OWN

"My teaching is not mine but his who sent me" (Jn 7:16). Jesus himself said these words. Imagine this. Not even the Son of God himself will claim responsibility for the teachings he imparts. They come from the Father and are then given to us.

Your teaching is not your own. It came from someone else. It came from your parents and grandparents. It came from teachers, preachers, catechists, and priests. It came from books and saints and faithful role models of the Christian life whom you looked up to for their Christian faith. The faith you hold was passed down to you like the flame of one candle passed on to the next.

Within the Catholic Church, all teachings have been passed down from one generation to the next through Sacred Tradition. Jesus Christ appointed Apostles, who appointed bishops by laying on of the hands, to pass on this Tradition and appoint their own successors. Through the power of the Holy Spirit, teachings and authority have been passed on through Apostolic Succession for centuries leading up to today.

Just as you received the Church's teachings from someone else as a gift, you will pass on this gift to another. To use our agricultural analogy, the seeds you sow are not your own. They come from another source. You plant the seeds, but the seeds were a gift given to you.

If these teachings are not your own, then don't take it personally when a student disagrees with you. Listen to the questions they have and address them as best as possible. Recognize that you are always trying to understand what we believe more deeply. The teachings you teach are not your own, so you can continue to learn along with the students, whose questions push you to go further in your own understanding. In the meantime, all you can do is teach what was given to you.

Just plant seeds. Pass on what you have been given.

# PRAY LIKE SAINT MONICA

Since we are just planting seeds and not responsible for the growth, what can we do? Do we just wash our hands and pass the buck to someone else? Do we separate ourselves emotionally and let fate take its course?

Of course not. Use Saint Monica as your model. She is well known, of course, for her tireless prayers for the conversion of her son, Saint Augustine. Do you know the full story?

Young Augustine came home one day and told his mother about his Manichaean beliefs. She was so angry that she kicked him out of the house! But then she had a vision in a dream of him dressed as a bishop. From that point forward, she dedicated her life to praying for and supporting her son with love.

But Augustine had other plans for himself. Instead of coming home, he ran away from Northern Africa and traveled to Rome. His mother found out and followed him there. He then fled to Milan and again his mother followed.

After seventeen years (yes, seventeen years!) of praying for her son, he finally experienced an encounter with Christ that led to his conversion. Guess whom he told first about his conversion experience: his mother, Monica.

Saint Monica provides an excellent model of acceptance of Saint Paul's reminder that "God gives the growth." Instead of trying to force her son's conversion, she turned to the Lord. She humbly accepted God's will and turned to him in prayer. She had plenty of seeds to plant, plenty of things to say, but she knew it was in God's hands. She kept praying for him every day with confidence in God's plan.

Pray like Saint Monica. Pray for your students because God is growing within their hearts a strong faith. Keep praying and smile about God's work in their lives.

Just plant seeds by praying like Saint Monica.

# APOLLOS TODAY

Who will be the Apollos in the lives of the students we teach today? Apollos was a Christian leader who remained in Corinth after Saint Paul left for another city. Saint Paul was with the Corinthians only for a short time just like we get to spend only a short amount of time with our students. We plant like Saint Paul until our students move on to the next grade and continue to grow up within the Church. We planted the seeds, but someone in their future will water their faith.

We can think of this watering as the mentoring all of us need to grow as disciples. It works best in a one-on-one relationship. As people grow more interested in their personal relationship with Jesus Christ, they need someone to help them navigate the choices they make and habits they develop. God gives the growth, but an Apollos remains by their side while the growth continues.

A religious educator like you can do the watering, but it usually occurs best in between the classes rather than in the classroom itself. It requires a long-term personal relationship with someone and the ability to answer questions and provide guidance along the way.

Parents and grandparents often do the watering. They walk with their kids along their faith journey. They set a good example and share their insights as the kids grow. Grandparents, especially, can offer their advice and life stories when it comes to faith. As a religious educator, you can jumpstart this mentorship between parent and child by telling the parents about their child's interests and development in class.

Coaches, who get the opportunity to work with young people for multiple years, often serve as mentors as well. They get to know kids on a personal level outside of the classroom. They get to walk with kids through life's challenges. If they have a strong faith in God, then they also get to serve as models of faith and mentors through their mentees' development of faith as well.

In today's Church, youth ministers often fulfill the role of watering in the lives of teenagers. Even kids in Catholic schools tend to have closer relationships with youth ministers in parishes as they get involved in retreats or service trips. These personal relationships open opportunities for growth. These youth ministers also empower teens as leaders to take ownership of their faith lives and help organize retreats and events for others.

As kids grow into adults, they start to find peers who will provide the watering. Within Bible studies or retreat teams, our students will someday find brothers and sisters in Christ who will be confidants and examples of faith. Pray that young people today are able to find these communities of disciples within which they can grow.

But what about you? You and I are planting seeds as teachers and catechists. Our students come in for a year and move on to the next grade and a new class next year. You might develop a relationship of trust and admiration with some of these kids. They may come back hoping for help and advice, and that is wonderful. There is always an opportunity to do some watering.

But for most of our students, we will just be planting seeds. It is important work. Someone else will build upon the foundation we set today. Most importantly, God will give the growth.

Just plant seeds and give thanks for those who will do the watering of these seeds you have sown.

# THE PARABLE OF THE CRACKED POT

If you do get the chance to be an Apollos for your students, keep in mind the Parable of the Cracked Pot. An Apollos is personally there along the journey of faith and waters the seeds that were sown. The role of watering and walking along the discipleship journey with someone holds a lot of responsibility, but the biggest mistake we can make is to try to be perceived as perfect.

Perfection coparates us from other Christians. We might want to seem like good people, but we really need to open our hearts and the wounds inside for other Christians to see it is a safe place to grow. If we set the expectation that growing in the Christian life is easy, then we run the risk of setting our students up for failure.

The ancient Indian Parable of the Cracked Pot will help you walk along the journey with young people. It has been told often within Christian settings because it expresses the ways in which God works through our weaknesses.

*Every morning a water bearer walked to a stream to fetch water. The water bearer carried the water in two pots on a wooden pole.*

*One pot was perfectly formed, but the other pot had a crack in its side.*

*Every day the water bearer traveled to the stream and back home, and every day half of the water in the cracked pot would leak out of its side.*

*The perfect pot was proud of its accomplishment. It did its duty flawlessly every day. It felt bad for the cracked pot for leaking so much water.*

*The cracked pot was full of shame. It felt like a failure.*

*Finally at the end of another failed trip, it apologized to its master. "I am so ashamed," it said. "I failed you and I'm not worthy to carry water for you. Please find a new pot to carry your water."*

*The water bearer responded with a smile, "Why are you ashamed? Look back upon the side of the path. What do you see?"*

*There all along the side of the path grew beautiful bushels of flowers. The flowers stretched from the house all the way to the stream.*

*The water bearer explained, "I knew about your flaw and we created something beautiful together from it. I planted seeds along the side of the path because I knew the water you held would allow those seeds to grow. Your brokenness brought so much beauty into the world! Thank you for being just the way you are."*

Saint Paul put it this way:

"Therefore I am content with weaknesses, insults, hardships, persecutions, and calamities for the sake of

Christ, for whenever I am weak, then I am strong" (2 Cor 12:10).

Let God be your strength. Don't be ashamed of your brokenness. Walk along the path with your students, never hiding the challenges that come with Christianity.

Just plant seeds by showing openness to your own weaknesses. If you get the chance to do some watering, then water through your wounds like the cracked pot.

# WHAT WON'T CHANGE?

Jeff Bezos, the founder of Amazon.com, shares some interesting insight into Amazon's philosophy. Amazon is well-known for its low prices and willingness to serve the customer with very low profit margins. They are able to keep these prices low because of their ability to think very long-term. Bezos framed his business with an interesting question. Instead of "what will change ten years from now?," he liked to ask, "what's not going to change ten years from now?" Are customers going to stop wanting low prices? Are customers going to want their packages to arrive more slowly? Of course not. So, they made those things priorities in Amazon's business model.

Let's apply this business model to religious education. What is *not* going to change in the lives of our students ten years from now? It is an important question to ask. We want the seeds we plant in their lives today to bear fruit a decade later. Therefore, what are we teaching that will still be just as relevant to a twenty-one-year-old as it is to an eleven-year-old?

A lot is going to change in their lives. They will change schools, teachers, technology, and hobbies. Life won't look the same for them.

What won't change? Think about the things that make us human. They will still worry about fitting in. They will still make mistakes and must learn from those mistakes. They will still have to overcome family issues and challenges. They will still be surrounded by people who pull them away from their faith.

This question may not apply to every lesson you teach, but it is important to ask. Again, what won't change? Are the lessons you teach still going to be important ten years from now? Are the seeds you plant going to be fruitful in ten years?

Just plant seeds that will be relevant a decade from now.

# JUST PLANT S-E-E-D-S

Our goal as religious educators is to plant seeds that will grow and bear fruit many years later. While we may not see the growth, we can concentrate on planting the right seeds at the right time. The remainder of this book offers some ways to plant the seeds that stick with our students for many years to come.

Here is an acronym to help you remember the five most memorable seeds to sow: SEEDS. Every time you teach or plan a lesson, keep the SEEDS acronym in mind. Use it as a checklist.

SEEDS stands for:

S - Stories

E - Emotion

E - Encounters

D - Discipline

S - Sayings

We will look in detail at each kind of seed and give specific strategies you can use in class. In the meantime, here is a brief explanation of the meaning of each word in the acronym.

S is for Stories

While we may have trouble remembering definitions we memorized in class, we can almost always remember stories. When we hear a story, we place ourselves in the shoes of the people in the story. Best of all, we reflect on the transformation in the story along with our own transformation. Then these stick with us. They become a part of us.

E is for Emotion

Teaching is essentially a transfer of energy and emotion. Passion is contagious. The more you love to learn and teach a topic, the more your students will want to experience that love as well.

E is for Encounters

Encounter is at the center of the acronym because it is the most important part of what we do. The experience of an encounter with our personal Lord and Savior is the single most important seed we can sow in the lives of our students. This meeting with the Lord will blossom into a lifelong relationship.

D is for Discipline

You can't spell discipline without disciple. Discipline is developed over time through hard work and practice. The Christian life consists of more than good feelings; it requires discipline to adhere to the commandments. As an educator, you will prepare students for the future by developing discipline today that becomes a part of who they are many years later.

S is for Sayings

All of us hear and repeat certain sayings that are so well crafted that they become impossible to forget. The Book of Proverbs and various other Bible verses offer great examples of these sayings. Years later your students might repeat one of your sayings, "I had a teacher that used to say . . ."

Let's dig into some ways to use these SEEDS in your classrooms this year.

Just plant SEEDS: Stories, Emotion, Encounters, Discipline, and Sayings.

# S IS FOR STORIES

# STORIES VS. ANECDOTES

There's a difference between a story and an anecdote. As a teacher you will share both anecdotes and stories, but it is important to know the difference. The seed of a story will find a place in the hearts of your students. An anecdote, however, might get repeated, but it won't be remembered. Your students might retell an anecdote once or twice, but it won't have a profound effect on them.

Here's the difference according to the book *How to Tell a Story*:

> "People tend to use the words anecdote and story interchangeably, but actually they are quite different. An anecdote is a short, amusing account of a real incident or person. A story is beyond a string of occurrences; it deals with evolution." (*How to Tell a Story* by The Moth)

The key difference in a story is the transformation. In a story, things change. A character goes on a journey and is transformed. A story doesn't have to be long, but it must include a story arc of transformation.

Here are a few examples to illustrate the difference. It should help you think of ways to turn your anecdotes into stories.

**Anecdote:** Mary Magdalene found an empty tomb, then Jesus appeared to her. Jesus had risen from the dead!

**Story:** Mary Magdalene and other disciples had lost all hope. On the third day after his death, Mary went to the tomb, but Jesus's body was gone! Then Jesus himself appeared to her and she was filled with joy. She ran to tell the other disciples the good news!

At the beginning of the story Mary was without hope, but by the end she was full of joy. The difference might sound subtle, but the story-version of this event is more powerful than the anecdote.

Here's another example:

**Anecdote:** When I was in high school, I experienced an encounter with Jesus Christ in the Eucharist. It was such a powerful experience, and it is the reason I am the person I am today.

**Story:** When I was a freshman in high school, I decided I didn't believe in God. I liked the people in my youth group, though, so I went to a summer youth conference. There I experienced a true encounter with Christ in the Eucharist. From that point forward, Jesus wasn't just an idea to me, he was a living God with whom I wanted to have a relationship. I went home changed and excited to share this relationship with others!

Both describe a change, but only the story shares what the actual change meant. This story is something someone can relate to, especially if they have had doubts about God. The anecdote is just something that happened.

Okay, one more example:

**Anecdote:** Saint Francis of Assisi is one of our greatest saints. He lived a life of extreme poverty and started a movement to rebuild the Catholic Church.

**Story:** Saint Francis of Assisi had a great life set out for him. He was going to inherit his father's successful business, and he was one of the most popular men in town. Then he experienced a call from God to live a life of poverty. When Francis shared his intentions with his family, his father disowned him, and he was publicly put to shame. Nevertheless, Saint Francis set an example for others, and his simple way of life and full dedication to God were hard to ignore. People started to join him and follow him, and news of his way of life spread throughout the world.

Again, the story is just a little bit longer, but without the transformation we are just sharing anecdotal facts. Get beyond the facts and share the transformation.

Just plant seeds by telling stories, not anecdotes.

# HOOK STUDENTS WITH STORIES

A story can be a great way to grab the attention of your students at the start of a lesson. From the moment your students sit down and you start teaching, their brains immediately start to wonder, "why do I have to learn this?" Sometimes the kids even verbalize this question. The best way to answer it is to share a story.

Every lesson needs a good hook. Just like every newspaper article needs a good headline. Every YouTube video needs a good opening. Every TV show needs an interesting opening scene. The creator of everything you read, watch, or listen to wants to grab your attention as quickly as possible. Or we might say they want to *hook* your attention like a fisherman hooks a fish.

Stories are my favorite way to hook attention. You can open up a lesson with a story and then constantly come back to the story as the summary of everything you are trying to teach. The layers of depth in the story will stay with your students long after they have forgotten what you said or what they did in class.

The fact is, stories stick. Ask kids what they remember about a homily after Mass. They might be able to muddle their way through a point or two that they heard, but I guarantee they will be able to summarize a story. The stories linger while the lessons fade.

Let's look at an example. Imagine you are teaching a lesson about the Trinity. What are some stories you could share at the beginning of the lesson and come back to as you delve deeper into an understanding of the Trinity?

You might recount some of these stories:

**Bible Story:** Share the story of Jesus's Baptism including the Holy Spirit as a dove.

**Saint Story:** Share a story about Saint Patrick teaching with the shamrock.

**Contemporary Story:** Share a video of a Catholic speaker's testimony about the Holy Spirit or Trinity.

**Fictional Story:** Share a summary of the Chronicles of Narnia story and its Trinitarian symbolism.

**Your Story:** Share a story of your experience with each person of the Trinity.

Pick the story you believe will best pique their interest. You also want to make sure the story is something you can repeat and come back to throughout the lesson. It helps to have props like a shamrock or dollar bill as well to use as a visual aid to the story. You can also use pictures as a reminder of your hook story.

Just plant seeds and grab their attention while you do it.

# THE FIVE SOURCES OF STORIES

Let's look in detail at five different kinds of stories you can share in class:

Bible Stories

Saint Stories

Contemporary Stories

Fictional Stories

Your Stories

# BIBLE STORIES

As Jesus said in his explanation of the Parable of the Sower: "The seed is the word of God" (Lk 8:11). If, therefore, the seed is the word of God, then it is important to ask ourselves how much do we read the Bible with our students? Furthermore, how much time do we dedicate to reflecting on the word of God in class?

The simple solution is to practice reading Scripture and practice simple Lectio Divina in class every time we see our students. Lectio Divina is a way of reading Scripture prayerfully to discern the word God is speaking to us in our hearts right at this moment. Let's look at how we can do a simple Lectio Divina in class.

Before we summarize the steps, I have to say one thing. Make sure you read the actual word of God with your students. You can definitely use the summaries in the textbook, retellings of the stories in books, printable resources, or online videos to help. But make sure you read the actual word of God. You never know which word or phrase will make an impact on their hearts.

There are traditionally four steps to Lectio Divina: read, meditate, pray, and contemplate. Some methods also include a fifth step: act. I find Pope Benedict XVI's summary of Lectio Divina in *Verbum Domini* to be the most helpful. After reading with your students, consider these four questions that accompany the four steps:

**Read**: What does the biblical text say in itself?

**Meditate**: What does the biblical text say to us?

**Pray**: What do we say to the Lord in response to his word?

**Contemplate**: What conversion of the mind, heart, and life is the Lord asking of us?

Follow these four steps when reading the word of God in class. Resist the temptation to only analyze and explain in the first step. Yes, you want to help the kids understand what they read. It is an essential first step, but if we want the seeds to be sown in their hearts, then we must invite them to meditate, pray, and contemplate the word of God.

Let's take the Parable of the Lost Sheep as an example. Follow the steps:

**Read**: What do we know about shepherds during Jesus's time?

**Meditate**: How are you similar to the lost sheep or to the 99 other sheep in the story?

**Pray**: As the lost sheep, what do you want to say to the Lord, our shepherd, who saves us?

**Contemplate**: As the lost sheep (or 99 other sheep), what is God calling you to change about the way you think and live?

The extra time it takes to meditate, pray, and contemplate can make a lasting impact on the lives of your students. You never know what God wants to say to them today. Instead of just learning about the Bible passage, help them to open their hearts to what God is saying to them today.

The seed is the word of God. Just plant seeds.

# SAINT STORIES

All of us need good role models in our lives. Thankfully, we can look to the past for better role models than we might have around us or that we might find in the media today. Some of the most successful people today spend time reading biographies and studying the greats in their field in order to improve themselves. The same should hold for people who seek to improve their spiritual lives.

We are blessed by a Church that highlights the lives of the saints who came before us. Rather than praising modern ingenuity when it comes to spiritual lives, we instead look to the past for role models in how to live today. The world changes, but humanity does not. The saints show us how to live.

The more you study the lives of the saints, the more you see how the saints that came before them were their inspiration. St. Ambrose gave St. Augustine a book about St. Anthony at a key moment in his conversion to Christianity. St. Ignatius, bedridden, found his heroes in a book about the lives of the saints. Think about the many saints named Teresa all recognizing the Teresas before them as inspiration: St. (Mother) Teresa of Calcutta, St. Therese of Lisieux, and St. Teresa of Avila.

Our students today need good role models of faith. It takes time to research and share the stories about the lives of the saints with our students, but it can go a long way in giving them models for how to live and get through difficult times. Share their full biographies and share their stories of transformation to inspire your students. Make it as relatable as possible and encourage them to think of ways they can relate to their relationships with God.

If it helps, think in terms of your students' Confirmation. They will pick (or have picked) a saint name for their Confirmation. Help them in this process by sharing the lives of many different saints. Mark their feast days throughout the year. Then, when they are Confirmed, they will have a large variety of role models to choose from for further inspiration.

Just plant seeds by sharing stories about the lives of the saints.

# CONTEMPORARY STORIES

We have sources of good stories all around us. As you come across an inspirational story on social media, in the news, on the radio, or in podcasts, save it for your class. You could use stories of the pope or other religious leaders, but you don't have to be limited to contemporary Church leaders. You might decide to feature athletes, musicians, celebrities, or people in the local news.

Again, the key is to make sure you share a story and not an anecdote to express a transformation. The kids can relate to a story and reflect on their lives. You can do this once again following the Lectio Divina format.

First, share the story and give the proper context and background to the events.

Then, invite your students to meditate on how their lives are similar to the person in the story.

Go one step further, asking them to talk to God in prayer about the transformation and the needs they have in their lives.

Then you can invite them to reflect on the transformation they need to make in their lives to do God's will.

These extra steps turn a contemporary story into a potentially life-changing experience. The seed of the story can turn into a new way of living for a young person.

Think about the lives of people today that have become an inspiration to you. Who are the athletes, celebrities, professional speakers, etc., whose lives have inspired a transformation in your life?

Chris Nikic, for example, was a huge inspiration for me and my family. Chris was the first person with Down syndrome to complete an Iron Man. Just a few months before his story made national news, our son was born with Down syndrome. We had a lot of uncertainties about his health and future at the time, but Chris's story filled me, my wife, and daughters with such great hope. Chris shares a message of getting 1% better every day to accomplish goals. That message stuck with us as we worked with physical, occupational, and speech therapists to help our son make small improvements each week.

A story can change your life. It can change the lives of your students.

Just plant seeds by sharing inspirational stories about people in the modern world.

# FICTIONAL STORIES

Most of the time when young people read or are taught to read, they are reading fiction. Parents read picture books to their kids at a young age. In grade school, kids check out chapter books and eventually novels from the library. Fictional stories hold an important place in the lives of young people today.

Therefore, fiction should have an important place in your classroom as well. You can draw from Christian-based fiction and Christian authors or make connections between our faith and more popular fictional stories. You can use picture books, fables, novels and novel excerpts, as well as TV shows and movies in class.

Fictional stories are popular because they enable us to have experiences we don't normally have on our own. Many kids love fantasy and science fiction or action movies and books because they can go on an adventure outside of normal everyday life.

When we integrate fiction into our lessons, our goal will be similar to all the other forms of storytelling we've discussed so far. Help the kids make connections between the characters in the story and their own lives. Help them put themselves in the shoes of a character and then learn from the character's experience. In this way, they personalize the stories.

We can do this with full-length novels and movies like *The Lion, the Witch, and the Wardrobe* by C. S. Lewis. There is a lot of Christian symbolism in this story, which is important to point out as religious educators. The real power of Lewis's book, however, is imagining ourselves as each one of the characters. When have you been like Edward or Peter or Lucy or Susan? How did each character relate to Aslan? How are these relationships similar to the way you think about Jesus Christ? The characters are the key to turning fictional stories into lifelong seeds.

You can also teach with short fictional stories like the "Footprints in the Sand" poem. The moral of the story is that God carried us during times of trouble so that only one set of footprints appear in the sand. To teach this story, we will want to encourage kids to imagine themselves in the story. When did they feel like God had abandoned them? How does it make them feel that it was during these times that God actually carried them?

Reflecting on these stories can have real power in the lives and hearts of the kids. Teaching them how to reflect on a story is a habit that can stick with them as they grow older. The story itself is a seed, but so is the way you teach them to read these stories.

Just plant the seeds of fictional stories and characters.

# YOUR STORIES

It is possible that the most important stories you share with your students are your own. You add a level of authenticity to your faith with stories about your relationship with God. Students only get to see you for a short time. Share your stories of testimony about who God is in this world. They will never get the chance to hear them again.

Why teach with testimony? Listen to what Pope Paul VI said about educators: "Modern man listens more willingly to witnesses than to teachers, and if he does listen to teachers, it is because they are witnesses" (*Evangelii Nuntiandi*, 41). If you want your students to listen, then share the stories of your authentic experience of faith. Make it real for them by sharing your life.

I'm a parent, and I always ask my kids about what they learned in school. Rarely do I get a description of an amazing lecture. Almost always I get a retelling of a story. Believe it or not, most of the time those stories are about the personal lives of their teachers. They love hearing about your life. They remember those stories. So, make sure you share stories about your relationship with God. It sticks with them.

Take a look at the next lesson you teach. Review all the things you want the students to learn. Now, think of a personal story of how you experienced that lesson in your life. Make it real for the kids. Share a story of transformation you experienced either big or small that will show them how important it is to learn what they will learn.

You are planting seeds, and the witness you share along with those seeds allows them to be planted deep in good soil. Share your story. Be a witness more than a teacher.

Just plant seeds with your authentic personal witness and testimony.

# E IS FOR EMOTION

# THEY WILL REMEMBER HOW YOU MADE THEM FEEL

"They may forget what you said, but they will never forget how you made them feel."

This phrase has been attributed to a variety of people, including author Maya Angelou. For obvious reasons it has been a source of inspiration for educators.

The fact is kids don't remember what we say in class. Sometimes they do and sometimes they don't. They might remember it tomorrow. They might remember it for their test. They might remember it months from now. But how about years or decades later? Will they remember your wonderful lecture?

Probably not.

But they will remember the way you made them feel in class. They will remember how your words of encouragement lifted them up. They will remember the inspiration you instilled in them by your actions.

Or heaven forbid they will remember how small they felt in your classroom. They might remember feeling alone and unwanted. They might remember feeling unworthy to be in your room and maybe even the Church.

Think back to the teachers in your life. How did they make you feel? Who left you with a good feeling? Who left you with a terrible emotional experience?

I have a vivid memory of breaking down in tears and crying in my mother's arms after a teacher yelled at me for a D on an assignment in second grade. I was scared to death of that teacher. I have no idea what that assignment was about or any other lesson she taught us in school. All I remember is the fear.

I also think back with gratitude for my high school English and history teachers. Both of them were passionate about what they taught. That passion was so contagious that it stuck with me into college when I changed my major to history and religion during my freshman year. I loved learning about those topics so much in school that I wanted to dedicate my life to that work. Those two teachers had a lot of memorable lessons, but it was the feeling of inspiration and love of learning that stuck with me for my entire life.

You get to choose the emotions you bring into class. Are you cultivating positive or negative emotions in the way you speak and interact with your students? You can also choose to be aware of the emotions your students might be experiencing at any given time. You cannot control how they feel, but recognizing the importance of emotions in class can really go a long way.

So, what feelings are your students walking away with?

Accepted or rejected?

Confident or afraid?

Proud or ashamed?

Inspired or bored?

Competent or dumb?

Make it a good feeling. They will remember the way you made them feel whether you like it or not.

Just plant seeds in their hearts with the memory of positive emotions.

# GET PUMPED UP

You've been to a sporting event, right? What happens before the game starts? There is usually loud music, lights, and a high-energy announcer getting the crowd excited about the game. Cheering and chanting heightens the level of emotion that crescendos into the kick-off, tip-off, or first pitch.

What about the players? They had a pregame pump-up routine as well. Many of them listen to music before a game. Their coach gives a pregame speech to fire them up as they head out of the locker room. They respond to the cheering crowds as they head onto the field or court with various emotional cheers.

Enthusiasm in education is just as important. As a teacher, you will pass on the energy and emotion you have about a topic. Through your teaching, you will transfer your emotion just like the emotion transfer between coaches, players, and fans.

So, get pumped up! Listen to music that gets you in the right emotional state. Read and meditate on an inspiring quote or Bible verse. Visualize the way you want the class to respond to what you have planned. Most of all, pray to get your heart in the right place before the students arrive.

Your emotion and energy are the seeds that will bear fruit in the hearts of your students. Get your head in the game, as they say. Get fired up and ready to make an impact.

Get pumped up and just plant seeds with your energy and enthusiasm.

# EMOTIONAL LESSON OBJECTIVES

At the top of every lesson plan, you should have two goals.

First, set a goal (or goals) for what you want your students to learn and be able to do with what they learn. Use the classic acronym "SWBAT", which stands for "Students Will Be Able To . . .", to start your lesson objectives, then pick a verb for what you want them to be able to do.

Students will be able to . . .

- identify, list, recite, describe, etc.
- summarize, paraphrase, explain, etc.
- categorize, compare and contrast, analyze, defend, etc.

Use this template:

SWBAT + Verb + topic (what you will teach)

But don't stop at educational objectives. You also want to think critically about the emotion you want students to have as they leave the room. They are not machines with heads you are filling with information. They have hearts, and we have an opportunity to light up those hearts with an emotional connection to the Lord.

Follow the same process. This time, use the abbreviation SWF for "Students will feel . . ." then pick an emotion you want them to have.

Students will feel . . .

- Happy: grateful for, joyful about, fortunate that, etc.
- Curious: interested in, concerned about, amazed by, etc.
- Blessed: content that, calm because, peaceful that, etc.
- Inspired: determined to, passionate about, energized that, etc.
- Love: affection for, compassion for, admiration for, mercy for, devotion to, etc.

Here are two examples.

**Topic: Confirmation & the Gifts of the Holy Spirit**

Students will be able to (SWBAT) list the seven gifts of the Holy Spirit.

SWBAT explain the meaning of each of the seven gifts of the Holy Spirit.

Students will feel (SWF) grateful for one of the gifts of the Holy Spirit in their lives.

**Topic: Crucifixion**

SWBAT summarize the story of Jesus Christ's crucifixion.

SWF admiration for Jesus's sacrifice on the Cross.

With an emotional objective you immediately see that changes need to be made to the way you plan a lesson. It is not simply enough for students to know what you taught, they must also feel something because of their experience in class. A summary of the Crucifixion is great, but actually feeling gratitude and admiration is our real goal in class. Knowing the gifts of the Holy Spirit will impress the bishop at Confirmation, but feeling gratitude to God for a gift will make the experience of the sacrament more memorable in their lives.

Set an emotional objective every time you teach. The intentional emotion turns your lesson into a seed that is sown and bears fruits in their hearts not just their heads.

Just plant seeds with intentional emotions in the hearts of your students.

# COMPLIMENT MORE THAN YOU CRITICIZE

It is remarkable how well children can cope with criticism and negative feedback. They hear it constantly from parents, coaches, teachers, not to mention their peers. All those negative comments stick with kids and over time they can solidify into a negative identity about themselves.

Psychologist John Gottman found in his research on relationships that we need five positive feelings or interactions with someone for every single negative feeling or interaction. Let's call this the "Magic Ratio" of positive feedback: five to one.

This much positive feedback can be quite a challenge. Can you provide five positive comments for every single negative comment or piece of feedback to your students? How about your own children, if you are a parent? Do you share five compliments for every one bit of criticism? It shouldn't be so difficult, but we fall into bad habits of criticizing more than we compliment kids.

Think about the children that struggle most in class. They are bombarded with negative feedback all day, every day.

They need someone in your position to give them praise no matter how small. This praise feeds into their confidence so they can develop a growth mindset.

Another psychologist named Carol Dweck defined the concept of a "growth mindset" versus a "fixed mindset." Someone with a fixed mindset believes they are dumb, smart, weak, strong, slow, fast, good, bad, etc. They believe these are fixed qualities they either have or not. But the truth is anyone can improve and get stronger, faster, and smarter. People who believe they can improve have a growth mindset.

When you praise your students' actions in a positive way, it cultivates a growth mindset. The problem is they receive so much criticism throughout their day that they develop a fixed mindset about themselves and their abilities. They hear criticism and it becomes their identity.

But you are planting seeds that grow into a growth mindset. You can give praise and good interactions to your students. You can praise specifically the good actions they do so they will want to repeat them again. They can then start to think differently about themselves because of the positive feelings you have given to them. Over time they will develop a new mindset of being able to grow, all because they received praise from you when no one else would give it to them.

Compliment more than you criticize. Just plant seeds of encouragement.

# BELIEVE IN THEM MORE THAN THEY BELIEVE IN THEMSELVES

Whether they show it or not, your students look up to you. What you say about them and what you do for them may stick with them long after they move on from your class. But nothing compares to the gift of confidence you can place in their hearts.

Believe in your students more than they believe in themselves. Every young person struggles with self-confidence. Even the outwardly confident kids are hiding their own insecurities. They need to believe in themselves, but they need someone else to believe in them first.

So many successful people today point to teachers, coaches, parents, and mentors, who saw something in them that they didn't see in themselves. While they didn't realize it at the time, that confidence planted a seed that flourished later. When they met adversity, they remembered that at least someone was in their corner.

You are that person. Be there in the corner for your kids.

They need you to believe in them especially when they fail. The kids that fail the most need your faith in them the most. Accept their failures and be confident in their ability to get past them. Give them hope when all hope is lost.

Through this simple belief in kids, we instill all three theological virtues. We practice love and connection with them despite mistakes. We give them hope when hope seems lost. We have faith in them so that they will have faith in themselves and, most of all, faith in God.

See something in them they cannot see in themselves. Believe in them more than they believe in themselves. Just plant seeds of encouragement in their hearts.

# E IS FOR ENCOUNTERS

# ENCOUNTERS EVERY DAY

It is possible that the phrase "religious education" is a misleading description of what we do. While we work in schools or parish education programs, the education must not be our primary goal. Our students will learn about the Catholic faith—there is no question about that—but a much higher goal exists in our classrooms and in the families of the kids we serve.

Pope Benedict XVI began his first encyclical with a phrase that has become central in Catholic faith formation ever since. He wrote:

> "Being a Christian is not the result of an ethical choice or a lofty idea, but the encounter with an event, a person, which gives life new horizon and a decisive direction" (*Deus Caritas Est*, 1).

His successor, Pope Francis, has echoed these words frequently throughout his papacy as have so many bishops and other Catholic leaders throughout the world. There is nothing more important than an encounter with Christ to create Christians in the world today.

No lecture can replace the power of an encounter.

No activity can replace the power of an encounter.

No lesson can replace the power of an encounter.

No story or idea can replace the power of an encounter.

It is an encounter with Christ that makes someone a Christian and nothing else.

Therefore, you must make time in every lesson for your students to have the opportunity to encounter Christ. I have frequently shared this vision for religious education:

*Every Day, Every Student, Every Class, an Encounter with Christ*

Recognize God's personal presence within your classroom. Always include the opportunity to encounter Christ with the religious education you provide. Every day should be an opportunity to listen and talk to the Lord.

Just plant seeds with the opportunity to have an encounter with the living God.

# ENCOUNTERS IN CLASS

An encounter with Christ can take many forms. The key is to give your students the chance not only to learn about Jesus but to come in contact with him. The shift in perspective is critical to transforming the lives of the people you serve.

Students can experience the presence of the living God through:

- the Bible
- prayers of petition
- prayers of thanksgiving
- prayers of praise
- sitting in silence
- reflecting on what they have heard or read
- listening to music
- experiencing Eucharistic adoration

Your classroom should be a different experience than anything else they see that day. You don't have to turn it into a chapel, but they should see it as a sacred space. Or, at the very least, there should be some reminder in the room of the sacredness around you: a cross, crucifix, pictures, paintings, statues, etc. These reminders set the tone to make the encounters more potent.

That same Lectio Divina process we used for stories can be applied to anything you teach. It is as simple as pausing to invite your students to meditate on what they have learned. In other words, they should ask God what he wants to say to them through what they have learned. It also means extending an invitation not just to say prayers, but to pray personally to the God who wants to speak to them today.

Pick an encounter. Personalize their prayers. Just plant seeds with meditation and prayer.

# ENCOUNTERING CHRIST IN THE CHURCH

Take a field trip. Go to the church (or chapel). I received an email once from a catechist who took her class to the church to pray. As they walked into the building, one of her students exclaimed, "I've never been in here before!"

Sadly, this experience has been shared among many religious educators. Set aside just for a moment the disappointment that families aren't going to Mass. Think about the opportunity here. We have the chance to give our students the uncommon opportunity to pray in the sacred space of our churches and chapels.

There is nothing quite like a quiet moment of prayer for a group of catechesis kids at night or in the calm in between Masses on Sunday mornings. If you haven't done it, then your students are missing out. I'm always shocked by how prayerful my students are when we visit the church. It often takes some reminding and setting a good example, but the space alone can set the tone.

Now imagine what this could do for them. Years from now, when life is taking its toll on them, will they find solace in a church? There will be times in their lives when they need Jesus. They will need hope and a touch of grace in their hearts. Deep in their memories, they might remember your trips to the church to pray. They might see a church, walk in, and remember the feeling they had of being there before.

Go to the church. Just plant seeds of invitations to pray.

# ARE YOU TRAINING THEM FOR TRIVIA?

Churches and schools love trivia nights. It's a great social event and fundraising idea. In Catholic churches and schools, trivia nights almost always have a category dedicated to Catholic teachings. It's fun to test people on all that catechetical knowledge they gained growing up in the Church, right?

I'll ask again: is this our primary goal? So many Catholic religious education classrooms seem to be dedicated to preparing kids to succeed in Catholic trivia. The term religious *education* can be misleading. Think about all that time spent memorizing definitions and listing the names of commandments, sacraments, and events in the Bible. You might have a class full of experts in Catholic trivia, but so what?

The problem is those Catholic trivia experts won't show up at a Catholic trivia night ten years from now unless they have a relationship with God. An encounter with Christ in class must be our highest priority. The encounter, not the education in trivia, is what will lead them into a dedicated relationship with Christ. Do not let the education get in the way of the encounter.

Does that mean we skip the teachings? Of course not. Let the education and the ideas they learn lead your students into a deeper encounter with the Lord. We must form young people in the Catholic faith by introducing the ideas we believe. It's important to give them that foundation of knowledge. We must make sure, however, that the knowledge is built upon the firm foundation of a relationship with God. That relationship can only occur through the frequent opportunities to encounter Christ.

Just plant seeds with encounters that lead your students into a deeper relationship with God. It is that relationship, not expertise, that will make a meaningful impact.

# GIVE SEED GIFTS

A physical gift can be a great way to plant seeds in the lives of the young people we serve. Author Brandon Vogt came up with a concept he calls "Seed Gifts." Seed gifts can be books, DVDs, CDs, pamphlets, or even prayer cards that you give now and see the fruits later. You might give them a book that sits on a shelf unopened or untouched for years. Then one day out of the blue, they might open it up and start reading. In that moment many years after the gift was given, an encounter with Christ can occur.

These gifts are true tangible seeds in their lives. You cannot predict what will happen after the gift is given. Remember, God gives the growth. He can use the gift however he pleases. He might inspire them to pick it up and encounter his son in a meaningful way long after they have left our classroom. It will be up to him either way.

I once received a Bible in one of my first catechesis classes as a child. I'm not sure if we were supposed to keep the Bibles or not. I didn't go to a lot of the classes that year, so I might have missed the time when they asked for them back. But ten years after my childhood religious education classes, I picked up that Bible for the first time in a meaningful way. By then I had encountered Christ in the Eucharist and I wanted to learn everything I could about him. I read that Bible so much that the spine frayed, and the cover eventually fell off. After lots of masking tape and then duct tape, I eventually got a new Bible for Christmas during high school. That first bible, whether intentional or not, was a seed that bore so much fruit many years later.

I know another educator who gives out saint medals at the end of the year. He selects specific saints for specific students and explains why that saint reminds him of each student. It's powerful. I worked with him one summer, and he gave me a double-sided saint medal with St. Joseph and St. Dismas. That gift solidified an identity I had always thought about myself. That small medal, and the small amount of time it took to personalize it, will be something that sticks with me and those students for many years and maybe for the rest of our lives.

Think about the gifts you can give to your students that might bear fruit later. Just plant seeds with gifts they will keep for years to come.

# D IS FOR DISCIPLINE

# DISCIPLINE AND DISCIPLESHIP

To become a Christian disciple, we must get beyond the good feelings we get from the love of God. As Jesus explains in his many parables, his disciples give up everything for the kingdom of God. As a response to God's love, we give up everything to love God back.

What does it take to be a disciple? Jesus puts it starkly: "If any wish to come after me, let them deny themselves and take up their cross daily and follow me" (Lk 9:23). Discipleship takes self-sacrifice. It takes will power and the discipline to accept suffering in order to love God and our neighbor.

As we make disciples in our classrooms, it is our responsibility to help develop the discipline and strength needed to take up their crosses. With a strong focus on stories and true encounters with Christ, we must also train our students to live out their faith.

As teachers, what are we training our students to do? Saint Paul wrote: "For the grace of God has appeared, bringing salvation to all, training us to renounce impiety and worldly passions and in the present age to live lives that are self-controlled, upright, and godly . . ." (Tit 2:11–12). We do this by correcting bad behaviors and challenging kids to give up the things that tempt them.

Let's not sugarcoat Christian discipleship. It requires our students to carry the cross. They are not alone in this suffering. We are there with them sharing our stories and continually giving them opportunities to encounter Christ. Then out of that emotional encounter, we challenge them to respond with self-sacrificial love for God and others.

Just plant seeds by taking up your cross daily.

# USE NEWTON'S FIRST LAW

Remember Isaac Newton's First Law of Motion from your high school physics class?

"An object will not change its motion unless a force acts upon it."

The First Law of Motion is sometimes referred to as the law of inertia. An object at rest will stay at rest unless a force moves it. An object in motion will stay in motion unless it is redirected by another force.

Let's apply this scientific concept to human nature:

A person will not change direction unless a force acts upon him.

As a teacher, you are that force. Our students will be on a certain path in life. When they encounter us, we can help redirect them to the right destination. There are so many temptations that will lead them astray in life. Everyone needs good role models and teachers to help see the right way to go.

Remember the story of Jesus calling the first disciples? They were fishermen, but he called them to become fishers of men. The disciples' lives completely changed direction because of their encounter with the Lord.

Discipline requires a clear direction. Sometimes discipline means finding a new direction in life. Always be vigilant. Ask yourself what path your students are on right now. What seeds can you plant to help them grow in a different direction? Your influence might be the thing they need most in life right now.

Just plant seeds and set your students on a better path.

# SET CLEAR CLASS RULES AND PROCEDURES

The rules and procedures you set up in class are more important than they seem. Yes, they will keep order in the classroom some or most of the time. You will have better behaved students with clearly defined rules and procedures for class. Clear expectations will also make your life easier.

Beyond the classroom management benefits today, however, is the long-term impact of clear rules and procedures. These directives are seeds planted now and practiced daily with the goal of bearing fruit many years later. Lining up in a single-file line, or turning in homework in a specific place, may seem like trivial procedures, but they train young people in discipline today that will help them remain disciplined later in life.

A few of the definitions of the word "discipline" refer to the necessity of rules. From Merriam-Webster's online dictionary, discipline is:

"control gained by enforcing obedience or order;"

"training that corrects, molds, or perfects the mental faculties or moral character;"

"a rule or system of rules governing conduct or activity."

A large part of what we do as educators is to train young people to be disciplined in their personal lives. For a habit of structure to take root, clear rules are essential. There should be no question about how to behave. Then discipline develops through the difficult yet habitual obedience to these rules.

If it sounds authoritative, then look to Scripture for clarity. It is no coincidence that the entire Old Testament is centered around God giving the Law to his people. Then, in the New Testament, Jesus reiterates the commandments but centers them on the virtue of love: "If you love me, you will keep my commandments" (Jn 14:15). The commandments require love and then lead us into love.

"Discipline equals freedom" as the popular podcaster and author Jocko Willink likes to say. We are slaves to sin and temptation, but the love of God frees us from that captivity. We are free by the disciplined adherence to the commandments. It is the "law of liberty" as Saint James wrote in his letter for "those who look into the perfect law, the law of liberty, and persevere, being not hearers who forget but doers who act—they will be blessed in their doing" (Jas 1:25).

Do not overlook the power of rules and procedures in class. Don't waiver on their importance and the clear enforcement of the rules you have established. You can correct behavior and encourage kids at the same time. By following your rules, they learn the discipline necessary to follow the Law of the Lord while also feeling your support as a trusted leader.

Just plant seeds with rules and procedures and enforce them with justice.

# PUNISH WITH A PURPOSE

Punishment isn't fun to talk about, but it is important. From time to time our students will act so far out of line that they must be punished. None of us enjoys enforcing punishment for disobeying rules, but it is important. There are natural consequences for actions. Our students must learn that natural consequences develop discipline in their lives.

All punishment must be administered with a purpose. Do not punish out of personal anger or retribution. The goal of every punishment is to teach a lesson. Punishment develops discipline. It must be directly aligned with the misbehavior.

Every punishment should accomplish two objectives:

1) Point out the unacceptable bad behavior.

2) Provide ways to avoid the bad behavior next time.

Therefore, the next time they are tempted to repeat this behavior, they will 1) fear the punishment and 2) know what to do differently.

Most punishments only attempt to achieve the first objective. Three strikes and you earn yourself a detention, for example. The kids and parents are upset, they serve their time, and then they go back to everyday life.

The key to punishing with a purpose, however, is to help a young person figure out what to do next time. Thinking through alternative choices to negative behavior takes time and effort on their part, but it is so crucial to the development of discipline in their lives.

First, clearly define the misbehavior and why it is bad. Then ask the students to come up with a better way to act or react next time. Don't just point out the problem. You must help them brainstorm the solution. As they accept the punishment, they should be thinking not only about what they did wrong but also what they should have done instead.

Therefore, stay calm. It's okay to be angry when someone misbehaves. Let the wrath roll off your back and remember the importance of punishment. The consequences are meant to correct the behavior, not just make them feel bad about what they've done. Once you separate yourself from the initial negative reaction, you can start to think critically about how to help a student change for the better. You want what is best for them, and the more they realize this desire to help, the more they will trust you and your guidance for how to change their behavior for next time.

Punishment today builds discipline for tomorrow. Just plant seeds with natural consequences and critical thinking about changes for the future.

# GIVE THEM THE GOLDEN RULE

Around the 17$^{th}$ century, English theologians started to use the term "Golden Rule" to refer to Jesus's teaching to "do to others as you would have them do to you" (Mt 7:12). The Golden Rule is set apart because of its universal nature. Nearly every religion and school of philosophy includes some version of this teaching.

The full quote, however, is important. Jesus said, "Do to others as you would have them do to you *for this is the Law and the Prophets*" (Mt 7:12). In other words, this rule summarizes the Old Testament. It is a simple saying and easy to remember and applies to most actions and temptations.

Jesus goes beyond the Golden Rule, however, by teaching his disciples the Greatest Commandments, which have a similar phrasing. "You shall love the Lord with all your heart and with all your soul and with all your strength and with all your mind and your neighbor as yourself" (Lk 10:27).

Love levels up the Golden Rule. Don't just treat others as you would be treated but love them as yourself. Put yourself in the shoes of others and love them as you would want to be loved. Jesus told the Parable of the Good Samaritan to illustrate this point. Be like the Good Samaritan who helps a dying man who was ignored by others.

What does the Good Samaritan story have to do with the classroom? Teach your students the Golden Rule. It's a universal principle to follow. Protect those who need to be protected in your classroom. Correct those who need to be corrected for failing to follow the Golden Rule. But most of all, do this with love, not anger or resentment.

A focus on love of neighbor will give your students a new direction. They need you to set them on the right path. They are going to be mean to one another and fall short of the Golden Rule. You must expect it, but don't accept it. Be direct in the way you want to raise the level of expectation in your class.

Just plant seeds of the Golden Rule with love.

# PRACTICE MAKES PERFECT WITH VIRTUES

The virtues guide our actions to do what is right. It isn't always easy to live out the virtues. They take practice. People need role models and teachers to help them live out the virtues, but you can't just explain a virtue. Knowing what a virtue is doesn't mean you will practice it when it counts.

Let's take the virtue of temperance, for example. You can teach about temperance and the need for chastity and abstinence. You can bring a chastity speaker into the school to inspire the students. You can give a series of lectures on the virtues of the theology of the body and the Church's teaching on sexuality. But ultimately, the only way to develop the virtue of temperance is to train someone to embrace it through practice.

You build virtue like you build a muscle in the gym. Lifting weights can cause pain as muscles are stretched, but if you accept that the pain has a purpose and habitually return to exercise, then the muscles grow stronger in recovery and repetitive work. The same goes for a virtue. Practice temperance by giving up something like candy. You experience the struggle, then grow stronger because of it. Then when the larger temptations arise, you have practiced the virtue already and built-up resistance to the temptations.

This moment of resistance is where you come in. Teach and practice the virtues. When you see a virtue in action, praise a student for it. When you see a vice in practice, redirect towards the better choice instead. Virtues are not easy. They require hard work and practice. Be the virtue coach they need to succeed.

Redirect to the right destination. Just plant seeds with virtues they can practice today and live out in adulthood.

# TEACH DOERS OF THE WORD

Saint James challenged his readers to "be doers of the word and not merely hearers who deceive themselves" (Jas 1:22). Our students will be immersed in the word of God in our classrooms. They will learn the Bible stories and meditate on the rich wisdom of the word of God. But they cannot stop there. They must act upon what they hear.

We will teach our young disciples how to practice discipline by becoming doers of the word, not just hearers in our classrooms. The natural next step of Lectio Divina (after reading, meditation, prayer, and contemplation) is *actio* (action), because God is sending us forth to live differently after we encounter him in his word.

Think of our work as being like that of a coach. Coaches draw up plays on a board in the locker room. Then the players go out and practice that play again and again until they get it right. All coaches know that players never execute a play perfectly the first time. It takes practice to live what they have learned.

The same goes for the spiritual life. When we hear the word of God, we must then go forth and practice. Practice and fail and try again until the day we die. To be a catechist like a coach, we help students practice the word in class in the way they speak and act. We give them tips on the challenges they will face along the way.

To be doers of the word we need discipline. You are there to help develop that discipline in class.

Just plant seeds so that they will be doers of the word not just hearers.

# SOW GOOD THOUGHTS

Ralph Waldo Emerson once said:

> "Sow a thought and you reap an action; sow an action
> and you reap a habit; sow a habit and you reap a
> character; sow a character and you reap a destiny."

The quote is almost Biblical and sounds a lot like Saint
Paul's warning: "You reap whatever you sow" (Gal 6:7).
We certainly want our students to develop good habits
and strong character. We want their destiny to be with God
in heaven.

So, let's break down this quote a little bit. If we want our
students to develop good character, then we must help
them develop good habits. The problem is we only see
them for a limited number of hours. Habits take a long
time to develop.

But during our one hour of class time a day or week (more
in elementary school of course), we can focus on their
actions. We can correct and redirect to better actions. We
can help them make better choices.

But even those opportunities can be limited. Therefore, we start at the beginning. Start with a thought. These thoughts will be a chain reaction from our classrooms to their destiny. Place within their heads, supported by their hearts, a thought that will reap better actions. Make your lessons as concrete as possible so they know exactly how to implement changes in their everyday lives. It may take some extra time to think about what is going on in the lives of young people today and how the lessons might relate to these experiences.

We cannot control the actions of our students outside of the classrooms, but we can help and coach along the way. We can plant seeds of an idea for how to live. Sow good thoughts so they will reap good actions. Let God give the growth and bring them to him in heaven.

Just plant seeds of good thoughts and reap good actions, habits, character, and destinies.

# S IS FOR SAYINGS

# THE "MY TEACHER USED TO SAY" TEST

Frodo Baggins's sidekick in *The Lord of the Rings* is Samwise Gamgee. He lives up to his name by sharing the many "wise" sayings from his father, Gaffer Gamgee. Frequently throughout their adventures in the book, Sam quotes his father with the phrase "as my Gaffer used to say."

He shares simple and memorable sayings like:

"Live and learn."

"It's the job that's never started as takes longest to finish."

"Where there's life, there's hope."

"Don't go getting mixed up in the business of your betters, or you'll land in trouble too big for you."

"All's well that ends better."

These sayings stuck with Sam through difficult times and offered key insights as the characters continued their journey.

Our students are on a journey, too. Wouldn't it be great if we gave them sayings like the old Gaffer's to constantly come back to for guidance?

Be the Gaffer! Gaffer is a word that can mean "old man." We need to be that old man in the memory of our students many years from now. Find your sayings and repeat and repeat and repeat them until they become unforgettable.

Years later we want our students to quote us: "as my teacher used to say." These sayings we share today will make an impact in their lives years later.

Just plant seeds with sayings they will never forget.

# MAKE IT PORTABLE

Andy Stanley is the leader of a megachurch in Atlanta. It's one of the largest churches in America. He is a very skilled preacher, podcaster, and author. He is known best for the simplicity of his messages. They are so simple, in fact, that he often gets criticized for lack of depth in his talks. He shrugs off the criticism because he knows it works. He's not talking down to his people; he is simplifying his message in a way they can easily remember.

He calls this approach his way of making a message "portable." A portable message is heard and then taken home. It is easy to remember and easy to share.

He didn't always preach this way. He once gave a talk to a group of high school students as a youth pastor. He just happened to come up with a phrase that he repeated frequently during the talk: "to understand why, submit and apply." Three years later one of the kids in that audience came up to him and quoted word-for-word the phrase he repeated during that talk: "to understand why, submit and apply." Three years later and the kid still remembered it! Stanley then made sure all his messages would include memorable phrases like that. Memorable is portable. Portable is memorable.

Here are some examples of the bite-sized messages I've written down from his talks, books, and interviews I've heard or read over the years:

"If it is mist in the pulpit, it will be fog in the pew."

"Be a church that unchurched people would like to attend."

"Control your money or your money will control you."

"People pray in one direction, but they walk in a different direction, and direction always determines where we end up."

"Direction, not intention, determines your destination."

"Leaders who don't listen will eventually be surrounded by people who have nothing to say."

Can you see how each of these phrases is easy to repeat and remember? The way the phrases are structured makes them memorable and memorable is portable.

As you prepare each lesson, think about a phrase you can repeat and get your students to take home with them. In the car ride home when their parents ask what they learned, will they have a phrase they can repeat?

Make your message portable. Just plant seeds with simple sayings your students will remember.

# REPETITION IS THE MOTHER OF LEARNING

As the Latin proverb says, *"Repetitio est mater studiorum,"* which means, "Repetition is the mother of learning." For many years repetition was the primary way to help students learn and memorize information. In recent years it has fallen out of practice, but its value should not be forgotten.

Motivational speaker Zig Ziglar took this proverb even further saying, "Repetition is the mother of learning, the father of action, which makes it the architect of accomplishment." Don't be afraid of repetition. In fact, you need to embrace it in class. The more your students hear frequently repeatable lessons and phrases, the more they will remember and repeat them. More importantly, as Ziglar said, these phrases will be implemented and put into action.

Think about the way catechesis was done in parishes and schools decades ago. Many people still remember learning from the *Baltimore Catechism* and its question-and-answer format:

*Q. Why did God make you?*

*A. God made me to know Him, to love Him, and to serve Him in this world, and to be happy with Him forever in heaven.*

Reciting this phrase might not take deep thought, but memorizing it sets the foundation to think more deeply. In times of reflection, when life gets confusing and disorienting, we need something to anchor us. From a Catholic perspective, what is the meaning of life? It's a big question. If you memorized the answer from the *Baltimore Catechism*, however, then you have a good starting point: God made me to know, love, and serve him.

As you embrace a few sayings yourself, make the commitment to recite and repeat them almost every time you see your students. If they get bored or roll their eyes, then good! That means it will stick with them for many weeks, months, and even years to come.

Just plant seeds and keep planting again and again and again.

# MAKE UP MEMORABLE MOTTOS

Okay, so how do you come up with your own sayings to share in class? Let's call these sayings "memorable mottos" to make the concept easier to remember.

What follows are five techniques to make up your own memorable mottos. These sayings will become seeds that bear great fruit.

Just plant seeds with sayings that use alliteration, rhyme, repetition, symmetry, and acronyms.

# ALWAYS APPLY ALLITERATION

Alliteration is the repetition of the first letter or sound of a group of words. Here are some familiar forms of alliteration you have probably heard before:

- Fish Fry
- Pitch Perfect
- Rocky Road
- Jump for Joy
- Busy as a Bee
- Live, Laugh, Love

The repetition of the beginning sound of each word makes it easy to remember and hard to forget. Use this repetitive sound to your advantage when coming up with phrases to teach.

Here are a couple of examples I have used in class:

"Mass means movement!"

The word "mass" comes from the closing words of the liturgy in Latin: "*Ite missa est*," which means literally, "Go, it is dismissed." Therefore, I like to challenge my students to think about these words and what they will do after the Mass. "Go!" In other words, "Mass means movement" so go forth and do something about what you experienced.

"Sin separates, the Savior reunites."

I like to explain to students that sin is essentially any action that separates us from God. Sin as separation comes as a surprise to some kids who only think about sin as breaking a rule. The difference helps them understand why Jesus is so important. He is the Savior and Redeemer. He saves us from sin and reunites us with the Father.

# IT'S RHYME TIME

A rhyme is a series of words or phrases that end with the same sound. A lot of poetry includes series of phrases that follow a consistent rhythm and end with the same sounds.

Here are some familiar rhymes that make a phrase easy to remember:

- High and Dry
- Rough and Tough
- Meet and Greet
- Shop 'Til You Drop
- Make or Break

Here are a couple of examples of rhymes in religious education:

"Jesus is the reason for the season."

This phrase is quite popular during Christmastime, right? It is a nice reminder that Christmas should be about Christ, not all the extra shopping, presents, etc. This phrase also comes in handy in catechesis in order to teach about all the liturgical seasons. Jesus is the reason for every liturgical season: Advent, Christmas, Ordinary Time, Lent, Triduum, and Easter.

"The bread and wine are fully divine."

The Eucharist isn't just an idea or a symbol. The bread and wine become the true body and blood of Christ. I like to repeat this phrase often in a lesson about the Real Presence. It is easy to get confused by all the terminology we introduce like transubstantiation, Real Presence, etc. I teach those terms, of course, but also give them the memorable motto: "the bread and wine are fully divine."

# REPETITION, REPETITION, REPETITION

Alliteration and rhyme are memorable because they repeat sounds at the beginning of the end of words. The same approach can be applied to a series of words or phrases using repetition.

Here are some examples you might recognize:

- I came; I saw; I conquered. (The original Latin has alliteration: "Veni, vidi, vici.")
- No pain, no gain (It rhymes, too!)
- Easy come, easy go.
- Out of sight, out of mind.
- Like father, like son.

In each of these phrases there is a word that repeats (I, no, easy, out, like), making it easy to remember. Use this repetition to your advantage when coming up with memorable mottos.

For example:

"Symbols show concepts, sacraments show Christ."

I used this phrase in a lesson about the sacraments. I wanted them to understand that Jesus Christ is present in the sacraments. They are not just reminders about him or explanations of what we know about him. We encounter Christ in the sacraments, and understanding the difference between a symbol (like a crucifix) and a sacrament (like the Eucharist) can go a long way.

# SIMPLIFY WITH SYMMETRY

We have talked about repeating sounds and repeating words, but you can also use a repetitive structure in your phrases. Symmetry in a phrase balances two ideas. "Symbols show concepts, sacraments show Christ" from the last example shows a balance of three words on each side of the comma.

Here are some other common examples:

- The bigger they are, the harder they fall.
- When the going gets tough, the tough gets going.
- The greater the risk, the greater the reward.
- What goes around comes around.
- You win some, you lose some.
- All for one, and one for all.

Here are many examples for religious education, all from the seventh chapter of the Gospel of Matthew:

"Do to others, as you would have them do to you." (Mt 7:12)

The Golden Rule is a great example of symmetry. It isn't perfect symmetry, but the repetitive structure makes it easy to teach and remember in class.

"Do not judge, so that you may not be judged" (Mt 7:1).

Again, this is not perfect symmetry, but the structure makes it more memorable. Why not judge? Because as Jesus then said: "For the judgment you give will be the judgment you get, and the measure you give will be the measure you get" (Mt 7:2).

"Ask, and it will be given to you; search, and you will find; knock, and the door will be opened for you" (Mt 7:7).

This is a great Bible verse to explain the importance of prayer:"____ and you will ____." The symmetry makes it memorable and easy to share. Prayer is like knocking on a door or searching for something you need.

These Bible verses are so much easier to remember because of the use of symmetry. It's sometimes easy to forget that the gospels were written decades after Jesus lived and died. His words were passed down by word of mouth through these years. Teachings like these were easy to remember and easy to share, which made it easy for the evangelists to include them in the Bible.

# A IS FOR ACRONYMS

Acronyms are a common method of making ideas memorable for teachers, speakers, and authors. An acronym is a word that is made up of the beginning letters of a series of words. Who is to say you can't come up with your own acronyms to make your lessons more memorable?

We use acronyms all the time in everyday speech, for example:

- ASAP (As Soon As Possible)
- LOL (Laughing Out Loud)
- FYI (For Your Information)
- DIY (Do It Yourself)
- FAQ (Frequently Asked Questions)

Acronyms can also be used as mnemonic devices, for example:

- ROYGBIV (Red, Orange, Yellow, Green, Blue, Indigo, Violet)

- PEMDAS (Order of operations in math: Parentheses, Exponents, Multiplication, Division, Addition, Subtraction)
- SMART Goals (Specific, Measurable, Achievable, Relevant, and Timed)

In religious education you might use an acronym like:

ACTS (Adoration, Contrition, Thanksgiving, Supplication)

While these words don't align exactly with the forms of prayer in the *Catechism of the Catholic Church*, the acronym ACTS makes it easier to remember that there is more than one type of prayer. Give your students the acronym and then explain the meaning of each word. It will be easier to remember the acronym and then think deeply about each kind of prayer.

# MEMORIZING CHAPTER AND VERSE

Here is one last idea for repeatable phrases. The ability of some Christians to recite Bible verses is quite admirable. Catholics are not well known for their ability to quote Bible verses, but for many Protestant groups, quoting Bible verses is engrained in their culture of Christian practice. They have studied, memorized, and repeated these verses so often that they can be applied to everyday life.

Do you have a particular Bible verse that is important to you? Saint Augustine did. When he read Romans 13:13–14, his life was transformed. He heard a voice saying, "Take up and read," then he turned to a random page in the Bible and read, ". . . let us walk decently as in the day, not in reveling and drunkenness, not in illicit sex and licentiousness, not in quarreling and jealousy. Instead, put on the Lord Jesus Christ, and make no provision for the flesh, to gratify its desires."

Saint Thérèse of Lisieux had a lifelong devotion to a particular Bible verse as well. In her autobiography, *The Story of a Soul*, she describes a spirituality of the Little Way, which was inspired by Matthew 11:25, which has Jesus praying, "I thank you, Father, Lord of heaven and earth, because you have hidden these things from the wise and learned and have revealed them to the childlike." By practicing the Little Way, we become like children and seek humble reliance upon God instead of recognition for great spiritual deeds.

Likewise, your students may be drawn toward certain Bible verses. These are not haphazard or coincidental occurrences. The Lord is pulling them toward these words. Students might copy them on a notecard or write them on sticky notes hung in their room. They might memorize and repeat the phrase in their heads or out loud.

These Bible verses are sayings that will stick with your students many years from now. Encourage your kids to select some of their favorite Bible verses. These verses may become a part of their identity like Saint Augustine and Saint Thérèse experienced. As you read the Bible with your students, focus on the memorable phrases that could inspire them.

Also, if you don't have a special Bible verse in your life, now is the chance to pick one. Are there any passages that have a particular interest to you? Read and memorize and think about the ways you can live out these words every day.

Remember, "The seed is the word of God" (Lk 8:11). Just plant seeds with Bible verses they will remember forever.

# A CONCLUSION: SOW THE SMALLEST OF SEEDS

At the end of this school year, you can look back on what you have done and tell yourself you did well. You planted seeds. Maybe you didn't see any impact. Maybe your students seem to be the same. But you know what? You did your duty. You planted seeds.

You shared stories.

You focused on emotion.

You gave them opportunities to encounter Christ.

You helped them develop discipline.

You repeated memorable sayings.

Remember, Saint Paul was the planter, and another person came along to do the watering. Most important of all, God gives the growth. We place all our work in his hands to cultivate and grow.

I'll leave you with a short reflection on a short parable about a small seed. Jesus said:

"[The Kingdom of God] is like a mustard seed, which, when sown upon the ground, is the smallest of all the seeds on earth, yet when it is sown it grows up and becomes the greatest of all shrubs and puts forth large branches, so that the birds of the air can make nests in its shade" (Mk 4:31–32).

Your work may seem small. It may seem insignificant in the larger scheme of the lives of your students. It's okay. It's true, your work is small, as small as a mustard seed. With these small seeds, God will grow a faith and love in the hearts of our students long after they have moved on from our classes.

Sow seeds, even the smallest seeds. Planting is our only responsibility. With joyful trust in God, we look forward to the next group of kids and a new opportunity to make small contributions to their lives.

Sow the seeds and let God give the growth. Let him turn the seeds we sow into the largest trees.

Just plant seeds.

# ABOUT THE AUTHOR

**JARED DEES** is the creator of The Religion Teacher (TheReligionTeacher.com), a popular website that provides practical resources and teaching strategies for religious educators. A respected graduate of the Alliance for Catholic Education (ACE) program at the University of Notre Dame, Dees holds master's degrees in education and theology, both from Notre Dame. He frequently gives keynotes and leads workshops at conferences, church events, and school in-services throughout the year on a variety of topics. He lives near South Bend, Indiana, with his wife and children.

Learn more about Jared's books, speaking events, and other projects at jareddees.com.

# ALSO BY JARED DEES

# ABOUT THERELIGIONTEACHER.COM

RELIGION TEACHER

TheReligionTeacher.com provides practical resources and teaching strategies for religious educators. Since Jared Dees founded The Religion Teacher in 2009, more than 100,000 catechists and religion teachers have used the website's lesson plans, activities, worksheets, and videos.

The Religion Teacher shares this vision:

*Every Day, Every Class, Every Student: an Encounter with Christ*

**The Religion Teacher Member Resources**

There are more than 1,000 downloadable worksheets and videos available to members of The Religion Teacher. To access these resources and opportunities for professional development, visit:

www.thereligionteacher.com